Holiday Jokes for Kids

Jokes for Easter, Halloween, Thanksgiving and Christmas

Sparky Riggs

FOREWARD

Humor has always played an instrumental role in my family and is something that still bonds us together. We can always seem to find the humor in life situations. It enhances everyday experiences and makes difficult situations more bearable.

Most of us think that someone is born with a good sense of humor, but the truth is that it can be learned and developed at an early age. Kids who develop a sense of humor can have a higher self-esteem, more resilience and live healthier, happier lives.

Keep on cracking those jokes!

-Sparky

CONTENTS

EASTER JOKES

What do you call a bunny with a large brain?

An egghead

What is the Easter Bunny's favorite vegetable?

Eggplant

What do you call an Easter Bunny with fleas?

Bugs Bunny

Why won't Easter eggs go out at night?

They don't want to get "beat" up

What's the Easter Bunny's favorite bedtime story?

A Cotton Tale

What do you call a rabbit that tells good jokes?

A funny bunny

Why did the Easter egg hide?

Because he was a little chicken

Why was the Easter Bunny so upset?

He was having a bad hare day

What do you need if your chocolate eggs mysteriously disappear?

An eggs-planation

What is the Easter Bunny's favorite kind of jewelry?

14 carrot gold

What do bunnies do when they get married?

Go on a bunnymoon

Where did the Easter Bunny learn how to ski?

The bunny hill

What happened after the Easter Bunny got married?

They lived hoppily ever after

How does the Easter Bunny travel on vacation?

On hare planes

Which bedtime stories does the Easter Bunny like most?

Hairy tales with hoppy endings

What day does an Easter Egg hate the most?

Fry days

What is the Easter Bunny's favorite sport?

Basket-ball

How does the Easter Bunny get off the highway?

He goes through an eggs-it

What did one Easter Egg say to the other Easter Egg?

Have you heard any good yolks today?

How does the Easter Bunny stay fit?

Eggs-ercise

Why wouldn't the Easter Bunny cross the road?

Because he's not a chicken

How does the Easter Bunny know where he buried treasure?

Eggs marks the spot

What kind of car does the Easter Bunny drive?

A hop rod

What is the fastest way to send a postcard to the Easter Bunny?

Using hare mail

What can you call the Easter Bunny when he has the sniffles?

A runny bunny

How do rabbits stay cool during the summer?

With hare conditioning

Why did the farmer feed crayons to his chickens?

He wanted them to lay colored eggs

How do you know when the Easter Bunny likes a movie?

Because he'll tell you it's egg-cellent

How does the Easter Bunny's day always end?

With a Y

Why is the Easter Bunny so lucky?

Because he always has rabbits feet on him

How does the Easter bunny stay in shape?

Hare-obics

How many Easter eggs can you put in an empty basket?

Only one – after that it's not empty

Why did the Easter Bunny have to fire the duck?

The duck was quacking the eggs

What do you get when you cross the Easter Bunny with a frog?

A bunny ribbit

Why did the Easter Bunny cross the road?

To get the chicken's eggs

What do you say to the Easter Bunny on his birthday?

Hoppy Birthday

What happens when you tickle an egg?

It cracks up

What does the Easter Bunny get for every basket he makes?

Two points, unless he's past the 3-point line

Why can't the Easter Bunny's ear be twelve inches long?

Because then it would be a foot

What kind of mistake does a ghost make?

A boo-boo

Why did the skeleton run away?

Because a dog was chasing after his bones

What does a ghost do when he gets in the car?

Puts his sheet belt on

How can you tell if a vampire has a cold?

He starts coffin

Why are there fences around graveyards?

People are dying to get in

Which kind of ship do vampires travel in?

Blood vessels

Are any Halloween monsters good at math?

No—unless you Count Dracula

What has hundreds of ears but can't hear a thing?

A cornfield

Why didn't the zombie go to school?

He felt rotten

Which fruit is a vampire's favorite?

Neck-tarine

Why didn't the skeleton jump off the roof?

He didn't have the guts to do it

How do you fix a damaged jack-o-lantern?

With a pumpkin patch

What do Italian ghosts have for dinner?

Spook-etti

What dog breed would Dracula love to have as a pet?

Blood Hound

Why is a cemetery a great place to write a story?

Because there are so many plots there

What do female ghosts use to do their makeup?

Vanishing Cream

Why didn't the skeleton do well at work?

His heart just wasn't in it

What's a witch's favorite subject in school?

Spelling

What did the mummy ghost say to the noisy young ghost who kept interrupting?

"Spook when you're spooken to"

What do mummies like listening to on Halloween?

Wrap Music

What would be the national holiday for a nation of vampires?

Fangs-giving

What is a monster's favorite dessert?

I scream

What position does a ghost play in hockey?

A ghoulie

What do you give a vampire when he's sick?

Coffin-drops

What kinds of pants do ghosts wear?

Boo-jeans

What do you get if you divide the circumference of a pumpkin by its diameter?

Pumpkin pi

What is a pumpkin's favorite sport?

Squash

Where do baby ghosts go during the day?

Day-scare centers

Why didn't the skeleton go to the dance?

Because he had "no" body to dance with

Why do ghosts hate the rain?

It dampens their spirits

THANKSGIVING JOKES

Why did the farmer run a steamroller over his potato field on Thanksgiving Day?

He wanted to make mashed potatoes

Why did the turkey cross the road?

It was Thanksgiving Day, and he wanted people to think he was a chicken

What is a turkey's favorite dessert?

Peach gobbler

Why did the cranberries turn red?

Because they saw the turkey dressing

What do you call it when it rains turkeys?

Fowl weather

Why do pilgrims' pants always fall down?

Because their belt buckles are on their hats

What is the saddest beverage on Thanksgiving?

Apple sighder

What kind of a jacket do you wear on Thanksgiving?

A harvest

What kind of "key" has legs and can't open doors?

A turkey

Why did the farmer separate the chicken from the turkey?

He sensed fowl play

What kind of music did the Pilgrims listen to?

Plymouth Rock

If pilgrims were alive today, what would they be known for?

Their age

What do you call a turkey on the day after Thanksgiving?

Lucky

Can a turkey jump higher than the Empire State Building?

Yes, of course! A building can't jump at all

Where did they take the Mayflower when it was sick?

The nearest Doc

What does Thanksgiving have in common with Halloween?

Gobble-ins

Who is never hungry on Thanksgiving?

The turkey because he's already stuffed

What kind of car brand would pilgrims drive today?

A Plymouth

What do you use to make Thanksgiving bread?

May flour

How did they clean clothes on the Mayflower?

They used Tide

What do pilgrim's learn in school?

Pilgrammar

If April showers bring May flowers, what do May flowers bring?

Pilgrims

What did the Mayflower sailors play when they were bored?

Cards – because they always had a deck

Why can't you take a turkey to church?

They use fowl language

What is a golfer's favorite Thanksgiving food?

PAR-tatoes

Why was the Thanksgiving dinner so expensive

It had 24 carrots

What's the sleepiest thing on Thanksgiving table?

The napkins

What's the smallest unit of measurement in the pilgrim cookbook?

A Pilgram

Where do turkeys go to dance?

The Butterball

Why do turkeys lay eggs?

Because if they dropped them, they would break

When does Christmas come before Thanksgiving?

In the dictionary

How do you make a turkey float?

Root beer, a scoop of ice cream and a turkey

Where did the Pilgrims put there trash?

In the Mayflower Compactor

What sound does a limping turkey make?

Wobble, wobble, wobble

What happened when the turkey got into a fight?

He got the stuffing knocked out of him

What was the turkey looking for at the toy store?

Gobbleheads

What sound does a space turkey make?

Hubble, Hubble, Hubble

How do you keep a turkey in suspense?

I'll let you know next week

Why did the turkey play drums in his band?

Because he already had drumsticks

What do you call an evil turkey?

Poultry-Geist

What did the turkey say to the computer?

Google, google, google

What do you call the age of a pilgrim?

Pilgrimage

What kind of tan did pilgrims get at the beach?

A Puritan

What did the Turkey say before it was roasted?

Boy, I'm stuffed

Why is the turkey such a fashionable bird?

Because he's always well dressed for dinner

What can you never eat for Thanksgiving dinner?

Breakfast or lunch

How many cooks does it take to stuff a turkey?

Only one, but you really have to squeeze them in

Why was the chef late to Thanksgiving dinner?

He lost track of thyme

Why was there a turkey on Comedy Central?

He was there for a roast

What do you call a turkey on the run?

Fast food

Why are so many cars sold around Thanksgiving?

Everyone wants an autumn-mobile

CHRISTMAS JOKES

What do fish sing during Christmas?

Christmas corals

What does Santa shout out at the start of a race?

"Ready, set, Ho! Ho! Ho"

What do you call Santa when he takes a break?

Santa Pause

Why did Santa have only eight reindeer last year?

Comet stayed home to clean the sink

Why was the little boy cold on Christmas morning?

Because it was Decemburrrrr

What do snowmen eat for breakfast?

Frosted Flakes

Why do mummies like Christmas?

Because of all the wrapping

What do you get if you cross an iPad with a Christmas tree?

A Pine-Apple

What does an elf use to spell?

The elfabet

What do you get if you mix a snowman with a vampire?

Frostbite

Why was Santa's little helper depressed?

Because he had low elf-esteem

What did the reindeer say to the football player?

"I'll be Blitzen you"

What is a bird's favorite Christmas story?

The Finch Who Stole Christmas

Where do snowmen keep their money?

In a snow bank

What is an elf's favorite sport?

The North-Pole vault

How do sheep say "Merry Christmas"?

"Fleece Navidad"

What did Adam say on the day before Christmas?

"It's Christmas, Eve"

What do you call a shark that delivers toys at Christmas?

Santa Jaws

What's the best thing to give your parents for Christmas?

A list of everything you want

What's the favorite Christmas Carol of new parents?

Silent Night

Where do mistletoe go to become famous?

Holly-wood

What is green, covered with tinsel and goes "ribbit ribbit"?

A mistle-toad

Why were the Christmas toys stressed out?

They already came wound up

What do snowmen take when the sun gets too hot?

A chill pill

What did the gingerbread man want for Christmas?

A cookie sheet

What do you call a greedy elf?

Elfish

What did one snowman say to another snowman?

"You're so cool"

What nationality is Santa Claus?

North Polish

What do street workers use at the North Pole?

Snow cones

What's Frosty's motto about his job?

"There's no business like snow business"

What does Santa need when he plays detective?

Santa clues

What's the difference between the Christmas alphabet and the regular alphabet?

The Christmas alphabet has NO-el

What does Christmas have to do with a cat lost in the desert?

They both have sandy claws

Where do polar bears vote?

The North Poll

What is a Christmas tree's favorite candy?

Orn-a-mints

What do people have who are afraid of Santa Claus?

Claus-trophobia

Why does Santa Claus like to work in the garden?

Because he likes to hoe, hoe, hoe

What do elves do after school?

Gnome work

What do you call an exploding Christmas tree?

A Tannen-Bomb

What do you get when you cross a bell with a skunk?

Jingle smells

Why did the gingerbread man go to the doctor?

Because he was feeling crummy

What is white, lives at the north pole and runs around naked?

A polar bare

How does Frosty the Snowman get around?

On an "ice"-icle

What kind of mug does a snowman use for lunch?

A frosted one

What do you call an elf who sings?

A wrapper

What kind of a bike does Santa ride in his spare time?

A Holly Davidson

What would you call an elf who just has won the lottery?

Welfy

What does Mrs. Claus say to Santa Claus when there are clouds in the sky?

It looks like rain, deer

How much did Santa pay for his sleigh?

Nothing. It was on the house

Why don't crabs celebrate Christmas?

Because they are shell-fish

Why does Scrooge love Rudolph?

Because every buck is dear to him

62707246R00046

Made in the USA
Middletown, DE
23 August 2019